Co-Parenting Journal
Tracking visitation and custody for divorced women and men

If you find this tracking journal helpful, please visit:

http://www.mentalhealthchampion.com

There you will find other books and articles to help with divorce and dealing with someone that may have a mental illness.

We have a complete series of books dealing with divorce and how mental health issues (narcissism, borderline personality, and bipolar) affect divorce and those having to deal with it.

A complete list of our Divorce Empowerment series can be found at:

http://www.mentalhealthchampion.com/books

The journal you hold in your hands is designed to be carried to any meeting you may have with your ex. During the meeting, whether that's to exchange the kids or discuss other issues, you will have this journal to record details before they are forgotten.

On each page you will find:

Date: Enter the date of the meeting - this may even be filled in ahead of time when scheduled

Meeting Time: The scheduled time of the meeting - this may be filled in ahead of time when scheduled

Time Arrived and Time Ex. Arrived: This is to record the time each party actually arrived, can be used to help show con-sistent tardiness

Meeting Place: the actual spot agreed upon to meet, public is better

Description of any incidents: the details of any problems you don't want to forget. This can also show consistent issues. Be warned, as many lawyers and judges will just view this as a He said/She said thing

Witnesses: this can be important as the details of any inci-dents can be verified

Filename of any pictures/videos: since it is a good idea to always be recording, if you've had problems, this will allow you to record the filename for future easy lookup

Feel free to use this journal as you desire. It is designed to easily fit in the glove box, a purse, or even a back pocket so that you can record any thoughts immediately.

We do not make any claim to legal or other advice. Please consult with a lawyer before relying on this journal during your divorce.

Date:

Meeting Time:

Time Arrived:

Time Ex. Arrived:

Meeting Place:

Description of any incidents:

Witnesses (name / contact):

Filename of any pictures/video:

Date:

Meeting Time:

Time Arrived:

Time Ex. Arrived:

Meeting Place:

Description of any incidents:

Witnesses (name / contact):

Filename of any pictures/video:

Date:

Meeting Time:

Time Arrived:

Time Ex. Arrived:

Meeting Place:

Description of any incidents:

Witnesses (name / contact):

Filename of any pictures/video:

Date:

Meeting Time:

Time Arrived:

Time Ex. Arrived:

Meeting Place:

Description of any incidents:

Witnesses (name / contact):

Filename of any pictures/video:

Date:

Meeting Time:

Time Arrived:

Time Ex. Arrived:

Meeting Place:

Description of any incidents:

Witnesses (name / contact):

Filename of any pictures/video:

Date:

Meeting Time:

Time Arrived:

Time Ex. Arrived:

Meeting Place:

Description of any incidents:

Witnesses (name / contact):

Filename of any pictures/video:

Date:

Meeting Time:

Time Arrived:

Time Ex. Arrived:

Meeting Place:

Description of any incidents:

Witnesses (name / contact):

Filename of any pictures/video:

Date:

Meeting Time:

Time Arrived:

Time Ex. Arrived:

Meeting Place:

Description of any incidents:

Witnesses (name / contact):

Filename of any pictures/video:

Date:

Meeting Time:

Time Arrived:

Time Ex. Arrived:

Meeting Place:

Description of any incidents:

Witnesses (name / contact):

Filename of any pictures/video:

Date:

Meeting Time:

Time Arrived:

Time Ex. Arrived:

Meeting Place:

Description of any incidents:

Witnesses (name / contact):

Filename of any pictures/video:

Date:

Meeting Time:

Time Arrived:

Time Ex. Arrived:

Meeting Place:

Description of any incidents:

Witnesses (name / contact):

Filename of any pictures/video:

Date:

Meeting Time:

Time Arrived:

Time Ex. Arrived:

Meeting Place:

Description of any incidents:

Witnesses (name / contact):

Filename of any pictures/video:

Date:

Meeting Time:

Time Arrived:

Time Ex. Arrived:

Meeting Place:

Description of any incidents:

Witnesses (name / contact):

Filename of any pictures/video:

Date:

Meeting Time:

Time Arrived:

Time Ex. Arrived:

Meeting Place:

Description of any incidents:

Witnesses (name / contact):

Filename of any pictures/video:

Date:

Meeting Time:

Time Arrived:

Time Ex. Arrived:

Meeting Place:

Description of any incidents:

Witnesses (name / contact):

Filename of any pictures/video:

Date:

Meeting Time:

Time Arrived:

Time Ex. Arrived:

Meeting Place:

Description of any incidents:

Witnesses (name / contact):

Filename of any pictures/video:

Date:

Meeting Time:

Time Arrived:

Time Ex. Arrived:

Meeting Place:

Description of any incidents:

Witnesses (name / contact):

Filename of any pictures/video:

Date:

Meeting Time:

Time Arrived:

Time Ex. Arrived:

Meeting Place:

Description of any incidents:

Witnesses (name / contact):

Filename of any pictures/video:

Date:

Meeting Time:

Time Arrived:

Time Ex. Arrived:

Meeting Place:

Description of any incidents:

Witnesses (name / contact):

Filename of any pictures/video:

Date:

Meeting Time:

Time Arrived:

Time Ex. Arrived:

Meeting Place:

Description of any incidents:

Witnesses (name / contact):

Filename of any pictures/video:

Date:

Meeting Time:

Time Arrived:

Time Ex. Arrived:

Meeting Place:

Description of any incidents:

Witnesses (name / contact):

Filename of any pictures/video:

Date:

Meeting Time:

Time Arrived:

Time Ex. Arrived:

Meeting Place:

Description of any incidents:

Witnesses (name / contact):

Filename of any pictures/video:

Date:

Meeting Time:

Time Arrived:

Time Ex. Arrived:

Meeting Place:

Description of any incidents:

Witnesses (name / contact):

Filename of any pictures/video:

Date:

Meeting Time:

Time Arrived:

Time Ex. Arrived:

Meeting Place:

Description of any incidents:

Witnesses (name / contact):

Filename of any pictures/video:

Date:

Meeting Time:

Time Arrived:

Time Ex. Arrived:

Meeting Place:

Description of any incidents:

Witnesses (name / contact):

Filename of any pictures/video:

Date:

Meeting Time:

Time Arrived:

Time Ex. Arrived:

Meeting Place:

Description of any incidents:

Witnesses (name / contact):

Filename of any pictures/video:

Date:

Meeting Time:

Time Arrived:

Time Ex. Arrived:

Meeting Place:

Description of any incidents:

Witnesses (name / contact):

Filename of any pictures/video:

Date:

Meeting Time:

Time Arrived:

Time Ex. Arrived:

Meeting Place:

Description of any incidents:

Witnesses (name / contact):

Filename of any pictures/video:

Date:

Meeting Time:

Time Arrived:

Time Ex. Arrived:

Meeting Place:

Description of any incidents:

Witnesses (name / contact):

Filename of any pictures/video:

Date:

Meeting Time:

Time Arrived:

Time Ex. Arrived:

Meeting Place:

Description of any incidents:

Witnesses (name / contact):

Filename of any pictures/video:

Date:

Meeting Time:

Time Arrived:

Time Ex. Arrived:

Meeting Place:

Description of any incidents:

Witnesses (name / contact):

Filename of any pictures/video:

Date:

Meeting Time:

Time Arrived:

Time Ex. Arrived:

Meeting Place:

Description of any incidents:

Witnesses (name / contact):

Filename of any pictures/video:

Date:

Meeting Time:

Time Arrived:

Time Ex. Arrived:

Meeting Place:

Description of any incidents:

Witnesses (name / contact):

Filename of any pictures/video:

Date:

Meeting Time:

Time Arrived:

Time Ex. Arrived:

Meeting Place:

Description of any incidents:

Witnesses (name / contact):

Filename of any pictures/video:

Date:

Meeting Time:

Time Arrived:

Time Ex. Arrived:

Meeting Place:

Description of any incidents:

Witnesses (name / contact):

Filename of any pictures/video:

Date:

Meeting Time:

Time Arrived:

Time Ex. Arrived:

Meeting Place:

Description of any incidents:

Witnesses (name / contact):

Filename of any pictures/video:

Date:

Meeting Time:

Time Arrived:

Time Ex. Arrived:

Meeting Place:

Description of any incidents:

Witnesses (name / contact):

Filename of any pictures/video:

Date:

Meeting Time:

Time Arrived:

Time Ex. Arrived:

Meeting Place:

Description of any incidents:

Witnesses (name / contact):

Filename of any pictures/video:

Date:

Meeting Time:

Time Arrived:

Time Ex. Arrived:

Meeting Place:

Description of any incidents:

Witnesses (name / contact):

Filename of any pictures/video:

Date:

Meeting Time:

Time Arrived:

Time Ex. Arrived:

Meeting Place:

Description of any incidents:

Witnesses (name / contact):

Filename of any pictures/video:

Date:

Meeting Time:

Time Arrived:

Time Ex. Arrived:

Meeting Place:

Description of any incidents:

Witnesses (name / contact):

Filename of any pictures/video:

Date:

Meeting Time:

Time Arrived:

Time Ex. Arrived:

Meeting Place:

Description of any incidents:

Witnesses (name / contact):

Filename of any pictures/video:

Date:

Meeting Time:

Time Arrived:

Time Ex. Arrived:

Meeting Place:

Description of any incidents:

Witnesses (name / contact):

Filename of any pictures/video:

Date:

Meeting Time:

Time Arrived:

Time Ex. Arrived:

Meeting Place:

Description of any incidents:

Witnesses (name / contact):

Filename of any pictures/video:

Date:

Meeting Time:

Time Arrived:

Time Ex. Arrived:

Meeting Place:

Description of any incidents:

Witnesses (name / contact):

Filename of any pictures/video:

Date:

Meeting Time:

Time Arrived:

Time Ex. Arrived:

Meeting Place:

Description of any incidents:

Witnesses (name / contact):

Filename of any pictures/video:

Date:

Meeting Time:

Time Arrived:

Time Ex. Arrived:

Meeting Place:

Description of any incidents:

Witnesses (name / contact):

Filename of any pictures/video:

Date:

Meeting Time:

Time Arrived:

Time Ex. Arrived:

Meeting Place:

Description of any incidents:

Witnesses (name / contact):

Filename of any pictures/video:

Date:

Meeting Time:

Time Arrived:

Time Ex. Arrived:

Meeting Place:

Description of any incidents:

Witnesses (name / contact):

Filename of any pictures/video:

Date:

Meeting Time:

Time Arrived:

Time Ex. Arrived:

Meeting Place:

Description of any incidents:

Witnesses (name / contact):

Filename of any pictures/video:

Date:

Meeting Time:

Time Arrived:

Time Ex. Arrived:

Meeting Place:

Description of any incidents:

Witnesses (name / contact):

Filename of any pictures/video:

Date:

Meeting Time:

Time Arrived:

Time Ex. Arrived:

Meeting Place:

Description of any incidents:

Witnesses (name / contact):

Filename of any pictures/video:

Date:

Meeting Time:

Time Arrived:

Time Ex. Arrived:

Meeting Place:

Description of any incidents:

Witnesses (name / contact):

Filename of any pictures/video:

Date:

Meeting Time:

Time Arrived:

Time Ex. Arrived:

Meeting Place:

Description of any incidents:

Witnesses (name / contact):

Filename of any pictures/video:

Date:

Meeting Time:

Time Arrived:

Time Ex. Arrived:

Meeting Place:

Description of any incidents:

Witnesses (name / contact):

Filename of any pictures/video:

Date:

Meeting Time:

Time Arrived:

Time Ex. Arrived:

Meeting Place:

Description of any incidents:

Witnesses (name / contact):

Filename of any pictures/video:

Date:

Meeting Time:

Time Arrived:

Time Ex. Arrived:

Meeting Place:

Description of any incidents:

Witnesses (name / contact):

Filename of any pictures/video:

Date:

Meeting Time:

Time Arrived:

Time Ex. Arrived:

Meeting Place:

Description of any incidents:

Witnesses (name / contact):

Filename of any pictures/video:

Date:

Meeting Time:

Time Arrived:

Time Ex. Arrived:

Meeting Place:

Description of any incidents:

Witnesses (name / contact):

Filename of any pictures/video:

Date:

Meeting Time:

Time Arrived:

Time Ex. Arrived:

Meeting Place:

Description of any incidents:

Witnesses (name / contact):

Filename of any pictures/video:

Date:

Meeting Time:

Time Arrived:

Time Ex. Arrived:

Meeting Place:

Description of any incidents:

Witnesses (name / contact):

Filename of any pictures/video:

Date:

Meeting Time:

Time Arrived:

Time Ex. Arrived:

Meeting Place:

Description of any incidents:

Witnesses (name / contact):

Filename of any pictures/video:

Date:

Meeting Time:

Time Arrived:

Time Ex. Arrived:

Meeting Place:

Description of any incidents:

Witnesses (name / contact):

Filename of any pictures/video:

Date:

Meeting Time:

Time Arrived:

Time Ex. Arrived:

Meeting Place:

Description of any incidents:

Witnesses (name / contact):

Filename of any pictures/video:

Date:

Meeting Time:

Time Arrived:

Time Ex. Arrived:

Meeting Place:

Description of any incidents:

Witnesses (name / contact):

Filename of any pictures/video:

Date:

Meeting Time:

Time Arrived:

Time Ex. Arrived:

Meeting Place:

Description of any incidents:

Witnesses (name / contact):

Filename of any pictures/video:

Date:

Meeting Time:

Time Arrived:

Time Ex. Arrived:

Meeting Place:

Description of any incidents:

Witnesses (name / contact):

Filename of any pictures/video:

Date:

Meeting Time:

Time Arrived:

Time Ex. Arrived:

Meeting Place:

Description of any incidents:

Witnesses (name / contact):

Filename of any pictures/video:

Date:

Meeting Time:

Time Arrived:

Time Ex. Arrived:

Meeting Place:

Description of any incidents:

Witnesses (name / contact):

Filename of any pictures/video:

Date:

Meeting Time:

Time Arrived:

Time Ex. Arrived:

Meeting Place:

Description of any incidents:

Witnesses (name / contact):

Filename of any pictures/video:

Date:

Meeting Time:

Time Arrived:

Time Ex. Arrived:

Meeting Place:

Description of any incidents:

Witnesses (name / contact):

Filename of any pictures/video:

Date:

Meeting Time:

Time Arrived:

Time Ex. Arrived:

Meeting Place:

Description of any incidents:

Witnesses (name / contact):

Filename of any pictures/video:

Date:

Meeting Time:

Time Arrived:

Time Ex. Arrived:

Meeting Place:

Description of any incidents:

Witnesses (name / contact):

Filename of any pictures/video:

Date:

Meeting Time:

Time Arrived:

Time Ex. Arrived:

Meeting Place:

Description of any incidents:

Witnesses (name / contact):

Filename of any pictures/video:

Date:

Meeting Time:

Time Arrived:

Time Ex. Arrived:

Meeting Place:

Description of any incidents:

Witnesses (name / contact):

Filename of any pictures/video:

Date:

Meeting Time:

Time Arrived:

Time Ex. Arrived:

Meeting Place:

Description of any incidents:

Witnesses (name / contact):

Filename of any pictures/video:

Date:

Meeting Time:

Time Arrived:

Time Ex. Arrived:

Meeting Place:

Description of any incidents:

Witnesses (name / contact):

Filename of any pictures/video:

Date:

Meeting Time:

Time Arrived:

Time Ex. Arrived:

Meeting Place:

Description of any incidents:

Witnesses (name / contact):

Filename of any pictures/video:

Date:

Meeting Time:

Time Arrived:

Time Ex. Arrived:

Meeting Place:

Description of any incidents:

Witnesses (name / contact):

Filename of any pictures/video:

Date:

Meeting Time:

Time Arrived:

Time Ex. Arrived:

Meeting Place:

Description of any incidents:

Witnesses (name / contact):

Filename of any pictures/video:

Date:

Meeting Time:

Time Arrived:

Time Ex. Arrived:

Meeting Place:

Description of any incidents:

Witnesses (name / contact):

Filename of any pictures/video:

Date:

Meeting Time:

Time Arrived:

Time Ex. Arrived:

Meeting Place:

Description of any incidents:

Witnesses (name / contact):

Filename of any pictures/video:

Date:

Meeting Time:

Time Arrived:

Time Ex. Arrived:

Meeting Place:

Description of any incidents:

Witnesses (name / contact):

Filename of any pictures/video:

Date:

Meeting Time:

Time Arrived:

Time Ex. Arrived:

Meeting Place:

Description of any incidents:

Witnesses (name / contact):

Filename of any pictures/video:

Date:

Meeting Time:

Time Arrived:

Time Ex. Arrived:

Meeting Place:

Description of any incidents:

Witnesses (name / contact):

Filename of any pictures/video:

Date:

Meeting Time:

Time Arrived:

Time Ex. Arrived:

Meeting Place:

Description of any incidents:

Witnesses (name / contact):

Filename of any pictures/video:

Date:

Meeting Time:

Time Arrived:

Time Ex. Arrived:

Meeting Place:

Description of any incidents:

Witnesses (name / contact):

Filename of any pictures/video:

Date:

Meeting Time:

Time Arrived:

Time Ex. Arrived:

Meeting Place:

Description of any incidents:

Witnesses (name / contact):

Filename of any pictures/video:

Date:

Meeting Time:

Time Arrived:

Time Ex. Arrived:

Meeting Place:

Description of any incidents:

Witnesses (name / contact):

Filename of any pictures/video:

Date:

Meeting Time:

Time Arrived:

Time Ex. Arrived:

Meeting Place:

Description of any incidents:

Witnesses (name / contact):

Filename of any pictures/video:

Date:

Meeting Time:

Time Arrived:

Time Ex. Arrived:

Meeting Place:

Description of any incidents:

Witnesses (name / contact):

Filename of any pictures/video:

Date:

Meeting Time:

Time Arrived:

Time Ex. Arrived:

Meeting Place:

Description of any incidents:

Witnesses (name / contact):

Filename of any pictures/video:

Date:

Meeting Time:

Time Arrived:

Time Ex. Arrived:

Meeting Place:

Description of any incidents:

Witnesses (name / contact):

Filename of any pictures/video:

Date:

Meeting Time:

Time Arrived:

Time Ex. Arrived:

Meeting Place:

Description of any incidents:

Witnesses (name / contact):

Filename of any pictures/video:

Date:

Meeting Time:

Time Arrived:

Time Ex. Arrived:

Meeting Place:

Description of any incidents:

Witnesses (name / contact):

Filename of any pictures/video:

Date:

Meeting Time:

Time Arrived:

Time Ex. Arrived:

Meeting Place:

Description of any incidents:

Witnesses (name / contact):

Filename of any pictures/video:

Made in the USA
Monee, IL
07 July 2026

56549106R00062